MW01634237

Comfort and Hope
for
Widows and Widowers

Comfort and Hope

FOR WIDOWS AND WIDOWERS

By Donnette R. Alfelt

FOUNTAIN PUBLISHING®

Fountain Publishing, P.O. Box 80011
Rochester, Michigan 48308.

Book design by Elisabeth Alfelt Eller
Set in Palatino and LTZapfino One
ISBN 0-9748423-3-8

Everyone knows that

a married pair who love each other

are intimately united

and that the essence of marriage

is the union of spirits or minds.

FROM EMANUEL SWEDENBORG'S *HEAVEN AND HELL*, NO. 375

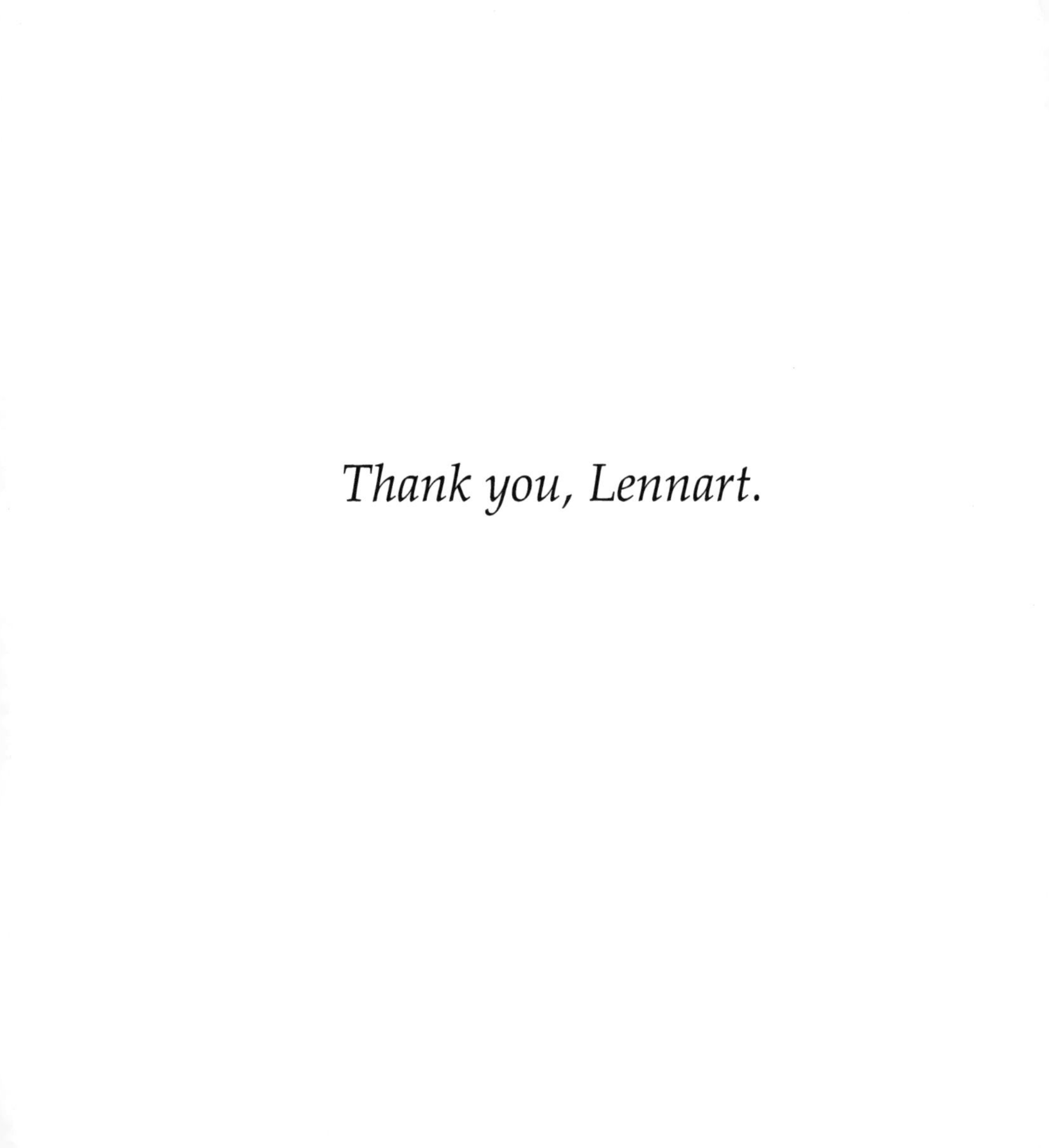

Thank you, Lennart.

Contents

INTRODUCTION

The following pages are, in part, from my experiences as a widow. An even more significant contribution has come from leading sessions for widows and widowers. Though mutual support through grief is part of the purpose of these groups, our primary focus has been looking to a reunion with our married partners in the next life. I thank all of these people who have shared with me and taught me. My thanks also to a variety of grief professionals with whom I have been associated.

As a member of the Swedenborgian New Church, I've gained comfort and hope from the works of Emanuel Swedenborg (1688-1772). He wrote extensively on the subject of life after death, and I have included many quotations from his works.

I use the term "conjugial love," found in Swedenborg's writings, to refer to true marriage love that looks to eternity.

My experience with friends from a variety of religions tells me that it is more common than not for those who love their deceased partners to believe they are still connected and that they will someday be reunited. In this booklet I touch on topics that have frequently come up with widows and widowers I have talked with over the past twenty years. My hope is that you will find something useful here.

"...they still do have sweethearts who make them smile — not because they were once in love but because they still are."

MITCH ALBOM, *PARADE MAGAZINE* 2/8/04 A STORY ABOUT WIDOWS AND WIDOWERS WHO BELIEVE THEY WILL BE REUNITED IN THE NEXT LIFE.

Not Separated

It's very difficult to live without the physical touch of a spouse who has died and to be unable to speak to him or her face to face. Many in our widows/widowers group do talk to their deceased husbands and wives in their minds or even aloud, and some find it helpful to write letters to them. I found that writing from my heart was an opportunity to express thoughts and feelings that I wasn't willing to share with others. I also discovered some feelings I had been hiding from myself.

Our husbands and wives also have things they would like to share with us from the perspective of their new life. A letter from a spouse might say something like the following:

"Peoples' souls and minds are not in a place like their bodies, because their source is heavenly and spiritual. And because they do not occupy space they can be joined together as if into one even when their bodies are not."

EMANUEL SWEDENBORG
CONJUGIAL LOVE 158

My Love,

Don't grieve for me. Bodies die but love does not. We all must live in an earthly body for a time, but this part of my life is over and real life is opening before me. I know that you miss my earthly presence, but be comforted by the knowledge that you are still part of my life because our spirits are still joined. I am not gone, but continue to dwell with you.

We are both being tenderly held by God, who understands our pain and will use our suffering as well as our achievements in marvelous ways that will contribute to our heavenly happiness.

The difficulties surrounding my leaving the natural world are now of no concern to me as I understand the bigger picture. Forgive me for my imperfections and mistakes. We both have regrets, but here things that once seemed important are put into perspective. As I see life more clearly in the light of eternity, my memory of upsets of life in the world dim and disappear while the

"When anything spiritual touches . . . something spiritual, it is the same as when something natural touches . . . something natural."

Emanuel Swedenborg
Heaven and Hell 461

true essence of our relationship grows stronger.

When you come over to the real world we will be reunited completely. Our love will then be unencumbered by earthly illness or concerns. Bodies suffer from aging and illness, but the spirit endures. You are not your body, nor was I. I am now in a world where my body is a true reflection of my spirit. The body I now live in is strong and young, free from the afflictions and limitations of the natural body I left behind. Though we can't touch physically, I continue to be touched by your love and the beauty of your soul.

Time on earth seems to go slowly, but in reality it is only a short time until you will join me. The beauty of the world I now live in is beyond what you can imagine. Your tears of sadness will be changed to tears of joy when I welcome you here.

Peace be with you until then.

*"You are joined at the heart
and always will be."*

GANGA STONE

Dreams and Visions

I feel a need to touch briefly on this topic. I recommend the book, *A Dove at the Window,* by Vera Glenn for more on the subject. She has recorded many uplifting accounts of widows and widowers experiencing the presence of their partners who are in the next world. Some of these came during sleep and others while awake.

Nine months after my husband died I was blessed with a dream about him that was different from any other dream in my life. It was more like a visit from him than a dream and it lifted me from a depressed state into one of comfort and optimism. I have had many more dreams about him but never another like this "visit." In widow/widowers groups over the years I have often heard from participants about special

"We are not human beings having a spiritual experience, we are spiritual beings having a human experience."

DR. WAYNE DYER

dreams and also of strong feelings of the presence of partners.

A most powerful account is found in Viktor Frankl's book, *Man's Search for Meaning*. Living through the horrors of a Nazi death camp—as he was forced to march when he could hardly stumble, hungry, sick and cold—he speaks of being with his wife when he did not know if she was dead or alive. He felt her with him, conversed with her and saw her "more luminous than the sun." He writes: "Love goes far beyond the physical person of the beloved."

It is a mystery to me why dreams and other experiences of a presence come to some and not to others. To say that they come to those who need them may be of little comfort to those who haven't experienced them or those who long for more.

I do believe that hearing these stories is reassuring to those who look for verification that life and relation-

"The essence of marriage is the union of spirits or minds."

EMANUEL SWEDENBORG
HEAVEN AND HELL 375

ships continue after death. However, there are other experiences that might not seem as remarkable, but which surely also come from the spiritual world. When you are touched by beautiful things of God's creation, from a sunset to a baby or a butterfly, you are feeling something that goes beyond the beauty that your eyes see. States of inspiration and peace come not only from things outside of you, but from things within, including the very real presence of loved ones who have died. These too are miraculous gifts from God. They are sometimes aroused by music, prayer, reflection or a variety of other means. They are as real and can be just as powerful as any of the dreams you hear about.

The message of all these experiences is that you are not alone. God is caring for you and for those you love who are in the next life and are still a part of you.

"Sometimes your grief can be overwhelming because it encompasses the grieving you never did for other, earlier losses in your life."

K.KATAFIASZ
GRIEF THERAPY

Grief

We are all visited by grief. It has been part of our lives since early childhood. The loss of a pet or a toy. The loss of a relationship or a dream. Some losses are forgotten and others continue to cause pain. This small book focuses on the death of a spouse. Knowing that the grief of this loss may be affected by previous losses in your life may help you to better comprehend the nature or depth of your sorrow. The more you understand the nature of grief and its meaning, the more likely you are to avoid additional trauma or complications.

Another factor that affects healing has to do with the grief of the people around you. Our adult children may be our best support, but in our needy state we may forget the significance of their loss and their needs. Also, stress can build when family members

"Earth has no sorrow that heaven cannot heal."

THOMAS MOORE

grieve differently. Some may seem uncaring because they feel a need to be alone or aren't inclined to share feelings. Others who grieve very openly may be helpful or may add to the stress. There is no way anyone can fully understand your grief, nor can you truly understand theirs. It is important to recognize these differences to avoid possible hurt feelings or conflicts that add to the pain. My five children reacted in very different ways when their father died. This added to my anguish, which I suspect in turn may have complicated theirs.

Young children who have suffered the loss of a parent or grandparent can also be distressed by your mourning. They may be upset to see you grieve, but in trying to protect them it is possible to do more harm. They need some protection, but the grief of adults should not be concealed from them entirely. They need reassurance and explanations even if they don't express their fears. If they are old enough to love they are old enough to grieve.

If it is a mother or father who has died, children may

"If you close children out, they'll come up with all kinds of misinformation about what's going on."

Lynn Caine
Being a Widow

become fearful that because the unthinkable has happened to one parent, it could happen to the other —a very frightening thought for a child. They need to understand as much as their age will permit about what has happened and what will happen next. They hear things and see things that they will interpret in their own way if no one takes time to listen and explain. Simple explanations such as "God needed Grandpa so He took him to heaven," may make a child wonder about a God who doesn't know or care how much they needed this person in their lives. "Grandma was so good she went to be with the angels." This may raise questions about the danger of being too good. "Grandma went to sleep and woke up in heaven" can generate sleep problems for a small child.

The loss of a spouse introduces a dramatic change in your life. First, there is an immediate need to take care of very practical matters and later, a loneliness when the funeral is over and the flowers have faded. Some of the people who have come to your aid and offered support

"Knowledge cannot erase the emotions accompanying grief, but knowledge can help us guide ourselves and each other toward recovery."

BERNADINE KREIS & ALICE PATTIE
UP FROM GRIEF

and love must return to their own lives and responsibilities. The time comes when you must reconstruct your
life and review your beliefs and direction.

You will need continued help from those close to you
and may need additional support and guidance from
other sources. As one widow expressed it, "We had
lots of visitors and support when he was sick. Now the
whole family is sick but the support isn't there."
Friends and family may be at a loss about how to
provide this support. Some may think they are doing
you a favor by distracting you with activities and
conversations that avoid references to your spouse. It's
as if they don't want to remind you of your deceased
partner. What they don't realize is that your husband or
wife is rarely out of your thoughts, and that it nourishes
you to hear that precious name and to know others are
thinking of your spouse, too.

It is the nature of grief to be unpredictable and undu-
lating. If you expect a steady climbing recovery you

"And God will wipe away
every tear from their eyes."

REVELATION 7:17

will be disappointed and discouraged. It is normal for life to be abnormal for a time. I recall times of peace when I felt at last I had made it through. I also remember these states being followed by relapses seemingly from nowhere or triggered by some small incident. There are uses served by the grief process, even in the tears. Tears of grief have ingredients that differ from tears of joy or laughter. This indicates that they have a special useful purpose that should not be denied. The phrase "a good cry" is understood by anyone who has had one. As much as we sometimes resist or even fight them, there is a change in us physically and emotionally after we let go and let the tears come.

In the Old and New Testaments are many passages that speak of grieving:

> "Blessed are they that mourn, for they shall be comforted." *Matthew* 5:4

> "I will not leave you comfortless." *John* 14:18

> "I will heal you of your wounds, said the Lord."
> *Jeremiah* 30:17

"God has not been trying to experiment on my faith and love in order to find out their quality. He knew it already. It was I who didn't."

C.S. LEWIS
A GRIEF OBSERVED

These passages and others acknowledge the necessity of mourning and the assurance of Divine help.

The Lord does not inflict or will your pain but will help you to survive it. God is not punishing or testing you. God is with you in your grief and will provide you with strength that may surprise you. The Lord will lead you to places where you can eventually recognize some good that may come from this temporary separation, and lead you in adjusting to this chapter in your life.

This time of loss is a vulnerable time when strong emotions can be disabling. Each of us will differ in the feelings we struggle with. Though anger is a common emotion at this time, it is not experienced by everyone. Guilt, self-pity, depression and others are also natural phases of grief that need to be experienced and expressed. It can be harmful to deny or suppress painful thoughts and feelings and it is not a sign of weakness to seek help in dealing with them. These are part of the process that will move you forward.

"God loves every person, and as He cannot do good to people immediately, but only mediately through people, He inspires people with His own love..."

EMANUEL SWEDENBORG
TRUE CHRISTIAN RELIGION 457.3

Grief is your ally, not your enemy. It is a process of emptying and rebuilding.

There are a variety of valuable resources available to the bereaved. The Lord works through people, and there are many good people to turn to: personal friends, family, professionals, and authors, to name a few. The One above all that you can go to directly is God. Reading, learning and praying in ways that bring you closer to God will also bring you closer to your partner. God's will is that you be in a joyous eternal marriage and it is God's desire to help you find your way.

With help from God and others, you may in time recognize emotions that are holding you back. Releasing them can allow room to feel the uplifting messages of the angels who are with you, and to more clearly feel the ongoing love of your spouse.

"Take your burdens of guilt to God and leave them with God."

WAYNE OATES

Guilt and Regrets

Feelings of guilt can complicate and prolong the pain of the grieving process long after the death of your spouse. Very often these feelings are inappropriate and unnecessary.

It is inevitable that there is confusion and stress in situations surrounding illness and death. There will of course be regrets regarding things done and not done, said and not said.

You are never held guilty for unintentional blunders. God, who is mercy itself, forgives our mistakes. Also, if your spouse could speak to you from the spiritual reality of the afterlife, he or she would put things into perspective for you. Your spouse, too, would forgive you.

It is also important that you forgive yourself. If you

"The 'if-onlys' can consume
you if you're not vigilant."

ALAN WOLFELT
*HEALING A SPOUSE'S
GRIEVING HEART*

feel guilt or regret, it is usually a sign that you did not intend to cause harm or that you wish you had better understood what to do or what was needed. There may have been times in states of exhaustion, fear or agitation when you acted in ways that you now wish you hadn't.

While feelings of guilt can be debilitating, feelings of regret can prompt you to do better in the future. You learn and you change, and can't continue to hold yourself guilty for past errors. If you wish you had been a better husband or wife, you can do this now by working to become the person you wish you had been. You can do this in anticipation of your marriage in heaven.

Each moment of your life is a new beginning. The Lord will walk with you as you move forward.

"Anniversaries and holidays — times that used to mean joy and celebration — can be among the toughest now. Observe them with care and simple ceremony to ease the pain."

K. KATAFIASZ
GRIEF THERAPY

Holidays and Anniversaries

Usually the first year after the death of a spouse is the most difficult. Grief counselors caution the bereaved about this. It is not a time to make major moves or decisions. Remarriage, a move to a distant place or selling the house may be impulsive attempts to heal. They may later be found to be the wrong decisions, arrived at from grief rather than reason. If such a change does seem reasonable it is well to seek the counsel of trusted family, friends or professionals. There are many grief groups, books and web sites that may also be helpful.

Part of the pain of the first year has to do with facing special anniversaries without your partner. These are times when the absence is felt intensely and when you know that nothing about the day will ever be the same

*"Grief drives men into habits
of reflection, sharpens the
understanding and softens
the heart."*

JOHN ADAMS

as it was. Your wedding anniversary, birthdays, Thanksgiving, Christmas and the date of your partner's death are all times that might bring up more acute pain. Planning to acknowledge these days in some way may ease this pain.

One woman in our group came from a culture where it is the custom to hold a party of remembrance on the first anniversary of a person's passing. I attended this and it seemed to me to be something we all should do. This could take away the angst for friends and family about just what they should or should not do on this day. It is also an opportunity for the bereaved partner to talk about and listen to words of love and appreciation for the one who is still so much a part of their own thoughts and feelings.

At the first Thanksgiving after the death, a family might begin dinner with each person saying something that they are thankful for about the missing family member.

Christmas, being a special religious and family holiday,

*"Wait for the L*ORD*; be strong and of great courage and He will strengthen your heart."*

PSALM 27:14

can be very difficult. I have heard of some painful experiences, but also of actions taken that diminished the pain and even brought joy to the day.

If you are to be with family you can make a point of bringing your partner into the day. He or she is on everybody's mind, and it is helpful to give the family some suggestions or direction. They want to do the right thing, but don't know what the right thing might be. A small remembrance can make a big difference. You may simply light a special candle or begin the day sharing memories or compose a special prayer for grace at dinner. You might also put together a memory gift for children, either young or old. This could be a framed photograph, a poem or some personal possession of their parent or grandparent. A letter to your children telling them some history or how you met and fell in love can be a gift to yourself as well as them.

You may or may not want to send Christmas cards the first year. Whatever you decide is the right choice.

"Some people elect to do something very different on the first Christmas without their loved one – something so different that the absence of the loved one won't be obvious."

HELEN FITZGERALD
MOURNING HANDBOOK

Christmas music may bring you peace or make you cry. In either case it can be beneficial.

The first Christmas after my husband died I wrote a poem for my children about their father's final days on earth. I gave it to them on Christmas eve and was alarmed when everybody began to cry. In my ignorance I thought I had done the wrong thing and remember apologizing and saying, "I didn't mean to make you cry." Of course I now understand how valuable that cry was for all of us. I also remember a happy Christmas following this emotional release.

At Christmas some choose to shop for gifts either from or for their partners. One widow bought a robe for her husband which she wrapped herself in on Christmas morning and later at other times when she wanted to feel close to him. Another used this season to have her husband's ring welded to her own as a promise of continued commitment. A special gift for the home that reflects a spouse's loves or qualities can be a lasting tribute. There are also beautiful ornaments to be

"Sometimes old holiday rituals are comforting after death and sometimes not. Continue them only if they feel good to you; consider creating new ones, as well."

ALAN WOLFELT
HEALING A SPOUSE'S
GRIEVING HEART

found. A special one might be bought in his or her memory to be hung and brought out again on future Christmases. A memorial tree or bush can be planted in the warmer months of the year. Watching this grow can be a reminder of the continuation of life. Consult your nursery for appropriate sturdy species.

When a special day approaches, do not choose to suffer or merely endure it. We use the birth dates of people in history who have made a difference to the world as a time to celebrate and remember them. Lincoln's birthday is not a day of mourning his loss but a day of appreciation for what he contributed to the world. Shouldn't we on the birthdays of our loved ones do the same? Celebrate and remember our partners contribution to our lives? Lincoln's spirit is alive, and our partners are even more alive to us.

Anticipating these dates can be worse than the days themselves. Choose to use the day in a meaningful way that would please your spouse. In this way you

*"Unable are the loved to die,
for love is immortality."*

EMILY DICKINSON

are more likely to feel his/her presence and to experience some satisfaction and even delight. Who this person was and what he or she loved can guide you to an activity that honors them while benefiting others. Something positive and special can be a gift to you and to others and a tribute to your marriage.

Remember that God is caring for your partner and for you and that He will be with you to guide you and to heal your wounds. He is with you in your joy and in your sorrow—in your faith and in your questions.

"Problems call forth our courage and wisdom; indeed, they create our courage and wisdom."

M. Scott Peck
The Road Less Traveled

The Absence of Grief

There are situations where the loss of a beloved spouse is not a cause for grieving. Usually this is because the process has, at least in part, already taken place. Grieving has come much earlier over a period of time as the mind and/or body of a spouse has deteriorated.

There is a grief process in accepting and adjusting to the loss of a partner as he or she once was. There is a necessary letting go of being able to communicate or truly be together, accompanied by physical and emotional challenges. There is also grief in the pain of witnessing the suffering of this person you love. When death does come, grief is tempered or may even be replaced by joy as the suffering ends. This is true especially for those who believe in life after death.

"...if God choose, I shall but love you better after death."

ELIZABETH BARRETT BROWNING

However, grief may revisit later as responsibilities of care-taking are over and there is time for reflection. There may then be an aching for the loss of what once was and a reliving of the difficult times, as well as the stress of the necessary practical things that must be taken care of. For older couples there may be an emptiness or impatience for the time when they will be reunited.

The barriers caused by serious illness are not unlike the barriers brought about by death. Both make it seem as if you are no longer connected to your partner. But at all times spiritual work continues as you do what you can to be true to your vows. There may be times you feel you have failed and times you feel at peace. The Lord does not require perfection, but provides fresh possibilities for progress with each new day.

"To spiritual eyes it is plainly clear that they cannot be torn apart by either's death."

EMANUEL SWEDENBORG
CONJUGIAL LOVE 321:6

Conjugial Love

I once heard this remark: "Having a husband or wife does not mean you are married any more than having a piano means you are a musician." This seems a bit harsh, yet I agree with its message. True marriage is more than a legal institution or a physical living arrangement. True marriage is an ongoing effort on the part of a husband and wife to grow closer to each other's hearts and minds.

"Conjugial love" is a term used by Swedenborg to describe true marriage love. His works describe it in several ways:

> "Conjugial love in its essence is nothing but the wish of two that their lives become one life."
> *Conjugial Love* 215

"Life is eternal and love is immortal, and death is only a horizon; a horizon is nothing save the limit of our sight."

ROSSITER WORTHINGTON RAYMOND

"Love belonging to the spirit, and to the body as a result of the spirit, is in the souls and minds of married partners, together with friendship and mutual trust."
Conjugial Love 162

"Conjugial love has the quality of each wanting to be the other's completely and reciprocally. When this is experienced they are in heavenly happiness."
Arcana Coelestia 2731

"Conjugial love is the fundamental love of all the loves of heaven and the fundamental of all the delights and joys of heaven, because every delight and joy is of love."
Apocalypse Explained 993.2

Some find this love on earth, and all who truly desire it find it in the world to come. This is an ideal that any person, married or single, can strive for by looking to the Lord and avoiding things that are contrary to it.

"The states produced by conjugial love are innocence, peace, tranquility, inmost friendship, complete trust, a mutual desire of mind and heart to do the other every good."

EMANUEL SWEDENBORG
CONJUGIAL LOVE 180

Since the process of conjugial love is a spiritual one, a husband and wife can grow in this true marriage love whether both are on earth, or one is on earth and one in the spiritual world. And, of course, when both are reunited after death, this love will progress with more power than we can imagine.

63

*"A human being is so created that
as to his internal he cannot die."*

EMANUEL SWEDENBORG
ARCANA COELESTIA 10591

The Eternity of Marriage
(Dwelling Together)

For a long time I have been familiar with this comforting number in *Conjugial Love* by Emanuel Swedenborg which is often read at memorial services in the New Church:

> "Those in true marriage love are not separated by the death of one because the spirit of the deceased dwells continually with the one not yet deceased until the death of the latter when they are reunited and love each other more tenderly than before because in the spiritual world."
>
> *Conjugial Love* 321

This was read at my husband's funeral and reiterated what had been part of our wedding ceremony when we

"Whatever spiritual qualities a person acquires in the world remain with him or her after death."

Emanuel Swedenborg
Heaven and Hell 349

pledged to look to eternity in our marriage. However, in the months following his death, as I struggled to get through each day, I could not feel this as a reality. I knew that thinking about him was not "dwelling" with him. Many of my thoughts about him were of his absence and were filled with fears, regrets and longing that made him feel more distant. Even recalling good memories about our life together was not dwelling with him in the present. I began to search for what this truly meant and how I might experience it.

We all may be able to separate those things that were obviously not part of our partner's true spirit and identify those that probably are. I began trying to separate the traits or characteristics of my husband that I felt were of his spirit from those which were of this world. I know that his integrity, gentle strength and kind heart are part of his true essence while his shyness came from things of this world. Other widows offered more examples. One spoke of her husband's rough exterior which hid a tender interior. She knew the tender heart was part of

"I am the resurrection and the life. He who believes in Me, though he may die, he shall live."

JOHN 11:25

his spirit while his rough exterior came from his father's example. Another told how she was anticipating a full reunion with her husband, now free of the alcoholism that divided them in their marriage on earth.

Characteristics based on fears, culture or family history may now be seen for what they were and what they were not. A spouse who had difficulty communicating or showing affection, or one who struggled with negative behaviors, is now in a place where these things can be understood and may be laid aside —by them and by us.

It is remarkable to hear how, after a period of time following the death of a spouse, many find they come to understand their spouses more clearly. Natural barriers that may have prevented a truly close connection are now gone. This makes it possible for widows and widowers to see their partners, themselves and their relationship more clearly.

Something else I have heard often from widows is their recognition of how they have grown or developed spiri-

"Our spirits are not limited by space and time. The spirits of loved ones remain together."

REV. GRANT ODHNER

tually since the separation. Some recognized they had been too dependent on their husbands and at first felt they would be unable to go on after his death. Yet, as months and years passed they learned that they could go on - not because they didn't really need their husbands but because they felt they were still together. One said, "I know I've become a stronger person and a better wife."

The most important work of any marriage has to do with the efforts of each to follow the Lord in honoring marriage. Most couples at any stage are not consciously "working on marriage" together. Rather, each individual is working on themselves for the sake of the other and of the marriage. This is still possible and meaningful as you avoid things that are destructive to the marriage and keep looking for ways to be a better person. On earth when your spouse was away or at work, the marriage was still there affecting the behavior and choices of each of you as you resisted things that were contrary to marriage and looked for ways to contribute to it. Conjugial love is the reward of each individual's spiritual

*"....love and thoughts are not
in space and time."*

EMANUEL SWEDENBORG
DIVINE PROVIDENCE 50

progress, and the death of one partner does not interrupt this process. If you love your partner and your marriage, your efforts to strengthen your relationship will continue. Your partner in the spiritual world is still part of who you are, what you want and where you are going.

Time as we know it is not a factor. Some fear that their partner's spiritual progress might go more quickly than theirs because they are in the spiritual world. If you reflect on this you will recognize that spiritual progress is not something married partners do in the same way or at the same rate even when both are on this earth. Though at times a couple may recognize areas where they have grown together spiritually, for much of married life each is traveling on his or her own spiritual path. Even with the marriage in mind, the journey is an individual one.

When you feel left behind, be confident that you are still on earth because God sees things you can learn or overcome that can best be done here. Also know that

"God has taken away the beloved and left us here for some purpose. There is work to be done, and people to be loved and helped."

HELEN KELLER

your partner is experiencing things in the afterlife that will best contribute to his or her spiritual progress. Be confident that your progress and that of your husband or wife will contribute to an eternal union.

There are husbands and wives still on earth that are apparently in very different situations. An extreme example might be when one is the caretaker and one has Alzheimer's. Even in these circumstances we can be sure that for both partners, essential spiritual work is going on. Nancy Reagan's devotion to her husband demonstrated her commitment to their marriage and to his true essence while his illness seemed to separate them. We can be sure their final years together on earth included a great deal of pain and frustration, and we can also be sure he is now whole and well and that they will be reunited.

After the accident that left actor Christopher Reeve paralyzed from the neck down, his wife, Dana, told him, "You are still you, and I love you." She was clear about her husband's essence. Now that he has gone on into the

"Even as we mourn, our loved ones are awake to the glories and wonders of new life."

Dennis Duckworth

next life, this essence still lives, and Christopher will continue to affect Dana and many others.

Even on earth, living together does not mean a couple is always truly dwelling together. In every marriage there are times of feeling close and times of feeling distant. As a widow I can testify that this continues. However, as the years pass the times of feeling close increase and become more comfortable as I feel a contentment and gratitude for my husband.

Doubts and fears during widowhood may arise as they do in all marriages. Most people who have been married for a long time remember times when they wondered if they had married their eternal partner. It is true that we cannot be certain, but it is also true that all of our efforts will contribute to our eternal marriage—even if it is with another.

If you long for and are interested in working toward a true eternal union you will find this in the world to come.

"The varieties and diversities in marriages...exceed all number."

EMANUEL SWEDENBORG
CONJUGIAL LOVE 324

Remarriage

After the death of a spouse, widows and widowers are free to marry again. There is no civil law or church law to prohibit this. As each freely chose to marry they are also free to remarry. For some this will be desirable and appropriate.

There are many considerations that must be weighed that are not in conflict with spiritual goals. We are told in the book, *Conjugial Love,* by Emanuel Swedenborg that because true married love is rare, and because even those in loving marriages have only "made steps toward it," all are once again in equilibrium after the death of a spouse. Some will wish to continue to work on the marriage that they are in, and others will find someone new to share their life with. Either of these choices can be made from a sincere desire to honor marriage and look to an eternal union.

"To feel the joy of another as the joy in oneself, that is loving."

EMANUEL SWEDENBORG
DIVINE LOVE AND WISDOM 47

No one can be certain that they are married to their eternal partner until the next life. Even so, all are asked to look to the Lord in their efforts to be a loving, faithful partner and to avoid things that are contrary to marriage. They may have honestly and sincerely tried to do this during their married life and after the death of one they can, if they choose, continue to do this in another marriage.

In the next life married partners are reunited and then are able to recognize the depth of their love. They then decide whether they will continue together as husband and wife or separate to find their true partners. On earth, after the death of one partner, many are able to see more clearly the true quality of their love and whether they feel inclined to marry another. Swedenborg's works also speak of very practical reasons for getting married again, including companionship and the care and raising of children (*Conjugial Love* 317-325).

"The LORD is good to all, and
His tender mercies are over all
His works."

PSALM 145:9

What you choose to do and the reasons why are very personal. Whatever decision a widow or widower makes in regard to remarriage should be honored and supported by others. No one else is in a position to make judgments unless there is evidence that inappropriate choices seem to be coming from a vulnerable state. It is recommended that those suffering a difficult loss be cautious when making such major decisions. Professional guidance may be necessary, or an honest consulting of trusted friends.

The happiness of eternal marriage is there for all those who wish and work for true marriage love. Life is full of change, but God is constant and merciful. With Him as The Guide you will find your way.

"And the LORD God said, 'It is not good that man should be alone."

GENESIS 2:18

A Question

What about *Matthew* 22:30?

> "For in the resurrection they neither marry
> nor are given in marriage..."

These words have been a stumbling block for many who know in their hearts that God created male and female with the intention that they complete one another. Jesus said "...what God has joined together, let not man put asunder," and that by marriage a man and a woman become one flesh or one person (*Genesis* 2:24). It follows that after death, if they truly love each other, they will still be together.

The above words in *Matthew* 22 seem to deny marriage in heaven. But look at the context of this question from

"So teach us to number our days that we may gain a heart of wisdom."

PSALM 90

the Sadducees. They asked about marriage in heaven even though they did not believe in heaven or a resurrection. They asked a hypothetical question about a woman whose husband had died. Tradition required that she then be given in marriage to her husband's brother. If this second brother were to die, they asked, and she were passed to a third brother, and so on through all seven brothers in that family, whose wife would she be in the resurrection?

The purpose of this question was not to learn about the afterlife, because the Sadducees did not believe in such a thing, but rather to trick and discredit Jesus. He silenced them with His response just as he had silenced the Pharisees that very same day, when they "plotted how they might entangle Him in His talk" (*Matthew* 22:15).

Jesus could not speak of heavenly marriage, a true union of souls, to people who saw a wife as a piece of property to be passed from brother to brother. The true answer to their question would not be something they could fathom. So Jesus told them a truth that referred to something else,

"There is a correspondence of married love with the marriage of the Lord and the church."

EMANUEL SWEDENBORG
CONJUGIAL LOVE 67

something the world would come to understand in time. In *Matthew* 22:30, Jesus is speaking of the spiritual marriage or union between God and human beings. Swedenborg explains, "The only kind of marriage meant here is spiritual marriage, and this clearly appears from the words that immediately follow, that they cannot die any more because they are like the angels and are children of God, being children of the resurrection. By spiritual marriage, union with the Lord is meant . . . and when it has been achieved on earth, it has also been achieved in heaven. Therefore in heaven the marriage does not take place again, nor are people given in marriage." (*Conjugial Love* 41)

As for marriages between human husbands and wives, Swedenborg writes, "When married partners love each other tenderly, they think of eternity in regard to the marriage covenant, and not at all of its being terminated by death." (*Conjugial Love* 216:4) God would not create this beautiful love only to take it away after death. Loving husbands and wives can feel this in their hearts.

*"Death is the end of a lifetime,
not the end of a relationship."*

MITCH ALBOM

A Suggestion

Find a quiet time and place to complete some or all of these sentences to your spouse. You may choose to do this in this book or in a separate journal.

I'm grateful you have been part of my life because...

A quality of yours that continues to affect me is...

A memory I treasure about us is...

I regret that...

"The LORD is near to all who call upon Him, to all who call upon Him in truth."

PSALM 145:18

I hope you know that...

The most difficult part of life without your physical presence is...

I think you might want me to...

I am trying to...

My prayer for today is...

93

"This life is only a prelude to eternity, for that which we call death is but a pause, in truth a progress into life."

SENECA

Closing Thoughts

You have suffered a severe emotional wound, and the healing will require time and attention. Parts of this book may speak to you and others may not. You may want to return to it after some time passes or go to other sources for the support you need.

You are a spiritual being who since birth has lived in two worlds. Your natural body makes it possible for you to function in this world while preparing for the next. Your spirit is also developing as you live this earthly life. Things of this world and of your spirit vie for attention, but it is your spirit that will live on. After you die and are reunited with your partner you will love each other more tenderly "because in the spiritual world." No longer distracted or divided by worldly concerns, you will be able to come together and to

"Death is simply a shedding of the physical body like the butterfly shedding its cocoon."

ELIZABETH KÜBLER-ROSS

know each other ever more intimately. Every day you are nourished by the spirits of all those you love in this world, near and far, and also by those you love who are in the next world. You can continue to delight in the spirit of your spouse and all those you love, and to experience their presence. Don't be disheartened if this doesn't come quickly or easily. You will come through this —you will smile again—you will heal.

About the Author

Donnette Alfelt describes herself as a happily married widow. Since the death of her husband she has explored the nature and value of grieving as well as looking for ways to continue to honor and work on her marriage. She served for a time as a bereavement counselor for Hospice. This led to her forming groups of widows and widowers who look forward to being reunited with their spouses in the next life.

She is the mother of five and grandmother of 13. Her first grandchild left this world when only eight years old, and Donnette looks forward to being reunited with her as well.

She is a retired teacher who taught high school courses focused on moral and spiritual choices in life. She also helped in the special education department and formed and directed a community service club in the school.

Donnette keeps busy with her grandchildren, leading the widow/widowers group, occasional teaching, editing a newsletter for an organization that serves families who have children with disabilities, and participating in a variety of other volunteer activities.

This little book is something she has wanted to do for a long time, knowing there are many who have lost a spouse who know that love lives after the body dies.

Donnette is also author of *Journal for Grief and Healing, When Someone You Love Dies.*

29229154R00058